Today, I asked God to remind you that you are deeply loved by Him. He's crazy about you, in fact!

"For God so loved the world that
He gave His one and only Son,
that whoever believes in Him shall not
perish but have eternal life."

JOHN 3:16 NIV

God's love did not begin at the cross.
It began in eternity before the world was established,
before the time clock of civilization began to move.

BILLY GRAHAM

For more inspiration, scan here:

Today, I asked God to give you a huge dose of His love—enough that it will spill over into all those around you.

Be devoted to one another in love. Honor one another above yourselves.

ROMANS 12:10 NIV

The more I remember God's love for me, the more I'll rest in that love.

AMBER C. HAINES

DaySpring

For more
inspiration,
scan here:

I prayed today that God's love would shine so bright in you that it will drive out any negative self-talk or hidden insecurities.

Many waters cannot quench love;
rivers cannot sweep it away.

SONG OF SONGS 8:7 NIV

Darkness cannot drive out darkness;
only light can do that.
Hate cannot drive out hate;
only love can do that.

MARTIN LUTHER KING JR.

DaySpring

For more
inspiration,
scan here:

Today, I asked God to richly bless you.

Walk in the way of love, just as Christ
loved us and gave Himself up for us
as a fragrant offering and sacrifice to God.
EPHESIANS 5:2 NIV

It is not how much we do, but how much love we put in the doing. It is not how much we give, but how much love is put in the giving.
MOTHER TERESA

DaySpring

For more
inspiration,
scan here:

Praying God will make all your fears disappear! God's love is so much bigger than anything that could be frightening you today.

There is no fear in love,
but perfect love casts out fear.
For fear has to do with punishment,
and whoever fears has not been
perfected in love.

I JOHN 4:18 ESV

Fear flees in the light of God's love.

BILLY GRAHAM

DaySpring

For more inspiration, scan here:

You can experience life's greatest blessing: loving others and being loved by them in return. I asked God to show you some examples of this blessing as you go about your day, so be on the lookout.

"Love each other. Just as I have loved you, you should love each other. Your love for one another will prove to the world that you are My disciples."
JOHN 13:34–35 NLT

Love God and He will enable you to love others even when they disappoint you.
FRANCINE RIVERS

DaySpring

For more
inspiration,
scan here:

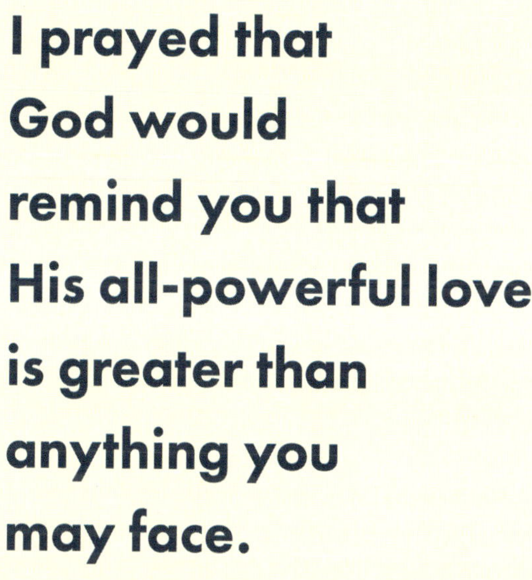

I prayed that God would remind you that His all-powerful love is greater than anything you may face.

We are more than conquerors
through him who loved us.
ROMANS 8:37 ESV

God's love never quits
or fails or walks away.
JENNIFER ROTHSCHILD

DaySpring

For more
inspiration,
scan here:

Today, I asked God to remind you that His love for you will never come to an end. It's a forever kind of love.

"Though the mountains be shaken and
the hills be removed, yet My unfailing love
for you will not be shaken nor My covenant
of peace be removed," says the LORD,
who has compassion on you.

ISAIAH 54:10 NIV

God's love is like an ocean.
You can see its beginning, but not its end.

RICK WARREN

DaySpring

For more
inspiration,
scan here:

I prayed for you just now, that God would bless you for the way you share His love with others. So many people are better off for knowing you.

"Give, and it will be given to you. Good measure, pressed down, shaken together, running over, will be put into your lap. For with the measure you use it will be measured back to you."

LUKE 6:38 ESV

Intense love does not measure, it just gives.

MOTHER TERESA

DaySpring

For more
inspiration,
scan here:

My prayer for you is this: that you come to see the difference you're making in this world, simply by loving others. It might not seem like much, but it's everything!

Let all that you do be done in love.

I CORINTHIANS 16:14 ESV

Not all of us can do great things.
But we can do small things with great love.

MOTHER TERESA

DaySpring

For more
inspiration,
scan here:

My prayer for you today is that God's love will give you the courage to keep going, keep giving, and keep believing. Love endures.

Love bears all things, believes all things, hopes all things, endures all things.

I CORINTHIANS 13:7 ESV

Our opinions are what we'll be known for; our love is what we'll be remembered for.

BOB GOFF

DaySpring

For more
inspiration,
scan here:

I asked God to remind you that you are adored by Him. In fact, you're His beloved child, a beautiful reflection of His love.

We love because He first loved us.

I JOHN 4:19 NIV

God is love. He didn't need us.
But He wanted us.
And that is the most amazing thing.

RICK WARREN

For more
inspiration,
scan here:

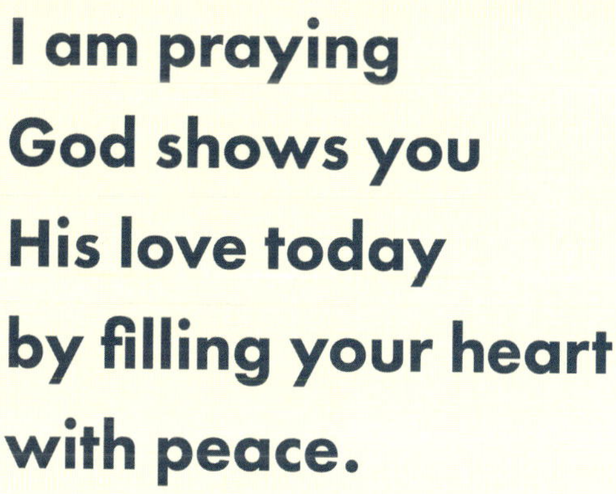

Don't worry about anything;
instead, pray about everything.
Tell God what you need, and thank Him
for all He has done. Then you
will experience God's peace,
which exceeds anything we can understand.
His peace will guard your hearts
and minds as you live in Christ Jesus.
PHILIPPIANS 4:6–7 NLT

Like a spring of pure water, God's peace in our hearts
brings cleansing and refreshment to our minds and bodies.
BILLY GRAHAM

For more
inspiration,
scan here:

God loves you so very much. I'm praying you experience the power of His heart today.

Meanwhile these three remain:
faith, hope, and love;
and the greatest of these is love.

I CORINTHIANS 13:13 GNT

In almost everything
that touches our everyday life on earth,
God is pleased when we're pleased.
He wills that we be as free as birds to soar
and sing our Maker's praise without anxiety.

A.W. TOZER

DaySpring

For more
inspiration,
scan here:

Today, I asked God to fill you with His love, letting it overflow to all around you.

Dear friends, let us love one another,
because love comes from God.
Whoever loves is a child of God
and knows God.
I JOHN 4:7 GNT

Our love to God is measured by our everyday fellowship with others and the love it displays.
ANDREW MURRAY

For more
inspiration,
scan here:

My prayer for you today is this, that you would be reminded that you matter greatly—to God and to others. His feelings for you will never waver.

Hope does not put us to shame, because God's love has been poured into our hearts through the Holy Spirit who has been given to us.

ROMANS 5:5 ESV

Though our feelings come and go, His love for us does not.

C. S. LEWIS

DaySpring

For more
inspiration,
scan here:

Look at you, doing hard things! Today, I prayed that God would remind you that He sees and He's so proud.

May mercy, peace, and love be multiplied to you.

JUDE 1:2 ESV

Faith makes all things possible . . .
love makes all things easy.

DWIGHT L. MOODY

DaySpring

For more
inspiration,
scan here:

I pray that God would remind you of the depth of His love for you—love that covers every trait you may see as an imperfection.

But each day the LORD pours
His unfailing love upon me,
and through each night I sing His songs,
praying to God who gives me life.

PSALM 42:8 NLT

I don't know how it works, the science and math of it all, but I know that love given is courage gained.

ANNIE F. DOWNS

For more
inspiration,
scan here:

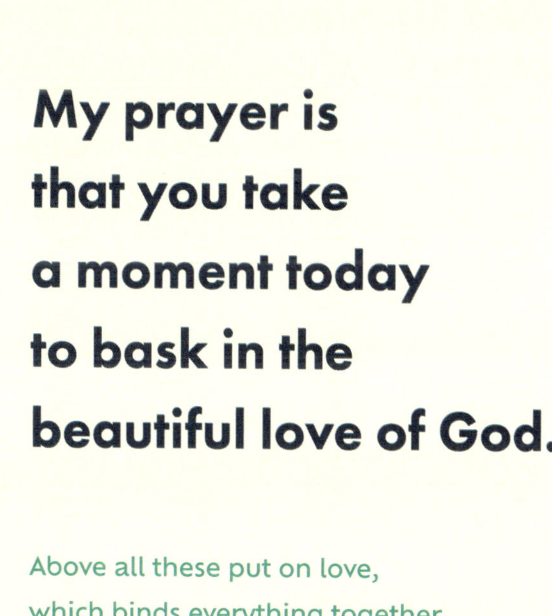

My prayer is that you take a moment today to bask in the beautiful love of God.

Above all these put on love,
which binds everything together
in perfect harmony.
COLOSSIANS 3:14 ESV

We love our earth. We love our people.
We love our stuff. We love our schedules.
We love our short lives here. And God is saying,
"Look up. This is going fast.
Your life here is barely a breath.
There is more, way more."
JENNIE ALLEN

DaySpring

For more inspiration, scan here:

Today, I thanked God for our friendship and the love we share. You mean so much to me.

Friends love through
all kinds of weather,
and families stick together
in all kinds of trouble.

PROVERBS 17:17 THE MESSAGE

We need people who can see our faces without makeup and our souls without scripts and our lives without the polish and practice.

HOLLEY GERTH

DaySpring

For more
inspiration,
scan here:

I asked God to remind you that His great love is bigger than any feelings of regret. He's got great things ahead for you.

You, my brothers and sisters, were called to be free.

GALATIANS 5:13 NIV

God never consults your past to determine your future. Dream big!

MIKE FRANCEN

DaySpring

For more
inspiration,
scan here:

I prayed that God would open your eyes to how truly beautiful you are.

Your unfailing love
is better than life itself;
how I praise You!

PSALM 63:3 NLT

Instead of looking outwardly and comparing yourself to others, look inwardly and see what you need to celebrate!

MELISSA HORVATH

DaySpring

For more
inspiration,
scan here:

I prayed that God would shine His light brightly on you today!

The LORD your God in your midst,
the Mighty One, will save; He will rejoice
over you with gladness, He will quiet you with
His love, He will rejoice over you with singing.
ZEPHANIAH 3:17 NKJV

The best and most beautiful things
in the world cannot be seen or even touched—
they must be felt with the heart.
HELEN KELLER

DaySpring

For more
inspiration,
scan here:

Today, I asked God to surround you with His love in such a deep and powerful way that it transforms your life in an incredible way.

I ask Him that with both feet planted firmly on love, you'll be able to take in with all followers of Jesus the extravagant dimensions of Christ's love.

EPHESIANS 3:14–19 THE MESSAGE

Beware of harking back to what you once were when God wants you to be something you have never been.

OSWALD CHAMBERS

DaySpring

For more inspiration, scan here:

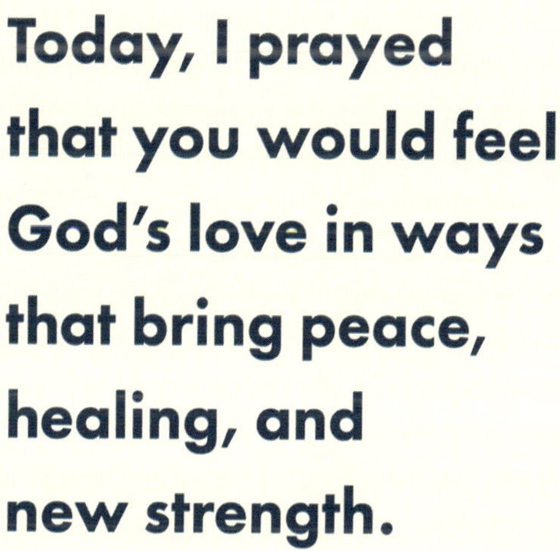

Today, I prayed that you would feel God's love in ways that bring peace, healing, and new strength.

"Peace I leave with you;
my peace I give you. I do not give to you as the world gives. Do not let your hearts be troubled and do not be afraid."

JOHN 14:27 NIV

When we recognize that God is the very present help we need, we can rest assured that He will give us the grace, patience, and love we need to handle life's challenges well.

JENNIFER GERELDS

DaySpring

For more
inspiration,
scan here:

I prayed that you would experience God's love in a powerful way today.

But he said to me,
"My grace is sufficient for you,
for my power is made perfect in
weakness." Therefore I will boast
all the more gladly of my weaknesses,
so that the power of Christ
may rest upon me.

II CORINTHIANS 12:9 ESV

God desires to work supernaturally
through normal people who are willing
to follow Him wholeheartedly and reflect His glory.

SALLY CLARKSON

DaySpring

For more inspiration, scan here:

God knows that you are facing choices today. And He sees that you are choosing to love, even when it's difficult. I pray that He will give you the courage to keep on loving.

Love must be sincere. Hate what is evil;
cling to what is good. Be devoted
to one another in love.
Honor one another above yourselves.

ROMANS 12:9–10 NIV

He measures our lives by how we love.

FRANCIS CHAN

DaySpring

For more
inspiration,
scan here:

God's love for you is real and authentic—it is a deep, unwavering love like no other. I prayed you'd be touched by this truth today.

May you experience the love of Christ.

EPHESIANS 3:19 NLT

Love is a fruit in season at all times, and within reach of every hand.

MOTHER TERESA

DaySpring

For more
inspiration,
scan here:

Today, I prayed for you to experience God's comforting embrace.

Do not be afraid or discouraged,
for the LORD will personally go ahead of you.
He will be with you; He will neither
fail you nor abandon you.
DEUTERONOMY 31:8–9 NLT

Every single thing you've been through
in your life has had a purpose.
BETH MOORE

DaySpring

For more
inspiration,
scan here:

I'm praying that God will wrap you in His love today—a love that is steadfast and unshakeable.

The faithful love of the LORD never ends!
His mercies never cease.
Great is His faithfulness;
His mercies begin afresh each morning.

LAMENTATIONS 3:22–23 NLT

Never be afraid to trust
an unknown future to a known God.

CORRIE TEN BOOM

DaySpring

For more inspiration, scan here:

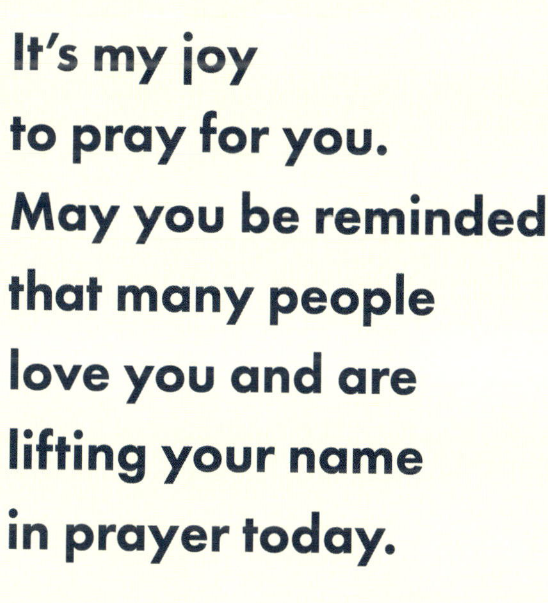

First of all, then,
I urge that supplications, prayers,
intercessions, and thanksgivings
be made for all people.
I TIMOTHY 2:1 ESV

There is nothing that makes us love a man
so much as praying for him.
WILLIAM LAW

DaySpring

For more inspiration, scan here:

You don't have to be strong. I asked God to be the solid ground beneath your feet today.

The Lord will be your safety.
He is full of salvation,
wisdom and knowledge.
Respect for the Lord
is the greatest treasure.

ISAIAH 33:6 ICB

When we believe, we find strength beyond our strength.

MAX LUCADO

DaySpring

For more
inspiration,
scan here:

I prayed and asked God to surround you like a warm blanket, filling every corner of your heart with peace.

The LORD gives strength to His people;
the LORD blesses His people with peace.
PSALM 29:11 NIV

The Christian does not think God will love us because we are good, but that God will make us good because He loves us.
C. S. LEWIS

DaySpring

For more
inspiration,
scan here:

I asked God to give you courage, and to reassure you of His presence in your life. He is with you today, strengthening you for whatever lies ahead.

God is love. When we take up permanent residence in a life of love, we live in God and God lives in us. This way, love has the run of the house, becomes at home and mature in us, so that we're free of worry.

I JOHN 4:18 THE MESSAGE

Gideon told God, "I can't," but God told Gideon, "You can because I have sent you and I will be with you." When you have Him you have all you need!

ROY LESSIN

DaySpring

For more inspiration, scan here:

Today, I asked God to calm all your anxieties and fears with His love and peace, which surpasses all understanding.

God did not give us a spirit that makes us afraid. He gave us a spirit of power and love and self-control.

II TIMOTHY 1:7 ICB

The chains of love are stronger than the chains of fear.

WILLIAM GURNALL

DaySpring

For more
inspiration,
scan here:

I prayed for you, that you could rest easy in God's love today. It's a wonderful place to be.

We know and rely on
the love God has for us. God is love.
Whoever lives in love
lives in God, and God in them.

I JOHN 4:16 NIV

O Lord, how happy should we be if we would cast our care on Thee, if we from self would rest; and feel at heart that One above, in perfect wisdom, perfect love, is working for the best!

HUDSON TAYLOR

DaySpring

For more
inspiration,
scan here:

Today, I thanked God for your kind, loving, and generous heart.

A sweet friendship refreshes the soul.

PROVERBS 27:9
THE MESSAGE

You are beautiful and beloved. And you are cherished, valued, vibrant, and here.

BONNIE GRAY

For more
inspiration,
scan here:

I'm praying God's unchanging love brings you hope today, offering comfort, guidance, and strength through life's ups and downs.

GOD is . . . right there with you.
He's right there with you.
He won't let you down; He won't leave you.
Don't be intimidated. Don't worry.

DEUTERONOMY 31:8 THE MESSAGE

He longs to quiet your heart with His love,
to calm your fears, insecurities,
and doubts with His presence.

RENEE SWOPE

DaySpring

For more
inspiration,
scan here:

You're like a flower in full bloom! I asked God to give you a clear picture of how His goodness and kindness radiate from you. You are beautiful in His sight.

Arise, shine, for your light has come,
and the glory of the LORD rises upon you.
ISAIAH 60:1 NIV

Since love grows within you, so beauty grows.
For love is the beauty of the soul.
SAINT AUGUSTINE

DaySpring

For more
inspiration,
scan here:

I'm praying for you today, that you would feel the warmth of God's love in every moment.

"For the mountains may move
and the hills disappear, but even then
My faithful love for you will remain.
My covenant of blessing will
never be broken," says the LORD,
who has mercy on you.

ISAIAH 54:10 NLT

God's love is unchangeable;
He knows exactly what we are
and loves us anyway.

BILLY GRAHAM

For more
inspiration,
scan here:

Today, I prayed for God's love to lead you to an understanding of the depth of His care for every fiber in your being.

Live carefree before God;

He is most careful with you.

I PETER 5:7 THE MESSAGE

The great basis of Christian assurance
is not how much our hearts are set on God,
but how unshakably His heart is set on us.

TIMOTHY KELLER

DaySpring

For more inspiration, scan here:

I'm asking God to give you peace as you take the next step in His plans for you. Rest assured, His plans are full of love and goodness.

"I know the plans I have for you," says the LORD. "They are plans for good and not for disaster, to give you a future and a hope."

JEREMIAH 29:11 NLT

God loves each of us as if there were only one of us.

SAINT AUGUSTINE

DaySpring

For more inspiration, scan here:

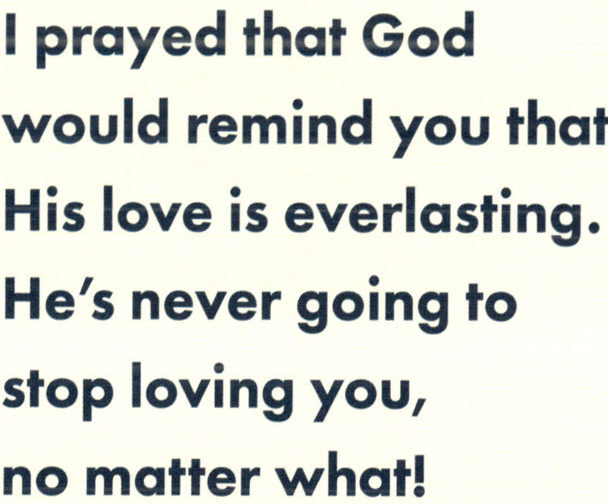

I prayed that God would remind you that His love is everlasting. He's never going to stop loving you, no matter what!

"I have loved you with
an everlasting love;
therefore I have continued
my faithfulness to you."
JEREMIAH 31:3 ESV

We know but little now about the conditions of the life that is to come. But what is certain is that Love must last. God, the Eternal God, is Love. Covet, therefore, that everlasting gift.
HENRY DRUMMOND

DaySpring

For more inspiration, scan here:

I asked God to lift the weight of the world from your shoulders. Remember, He's got this.

"Come to Me, all of you who are weary
and carry heavy burdens,
and I will give you rest."

MATTHEW 11:28 NLT

When you accept the fact that
sometimes seasons are dry and times are hard
and that God is in control of both,
you will discover a sense of divine refuge,
because the hope then is in God and not in yourself.

CHUCK SWINDOLL

DaySpring

For more inspiration, scan here:

I prayed that God would shower you with blessings today.

May the LORD bless you and protect you.
May the LORD smile on you
and be gracious to you.
May the LORD show you His favor
and give you His peace.
NUMBERS 6:24–26 NLT

However many blessings we expect from God, His infinite liberality will always exceed all our wishes and our thoughts.
JOHN CALVIN

I prayed for you today. When doubt or insecurity sets in, I hope you know that God sees you through the eyes of love.

For we are God's handiwork,
created in Christ Jesus
to do good works,
which God prepared
in advance for us to do.
EPHESIANS 2:10 NIV

Faith is a living, daring confidence in God's grace, so sure and certain that a man could stake his life on it a thousand times.
MARTIN LUTHER

DaySpring

For more
inspiration,
scan here:

Loving and being loved are the two greatest blessings. Today, I prayed that God would show You how very much You are loved—by Him and others—and what a blessing you are when you share that love with those around you.

And he said to him, "You shall love the Lord your God with all your heart and with all your soul and with all your mind. This is the great and first commandment. And a second is like it: You shall love your neighbor as yourself."
MATTHEW 22:37–39 ESV

Being loved is life's second greatest blessing;
loving is the greatest.
JACK HYLES

For more
inspiration,
scan here:

God made you with a beauty that shines not only on the outside, but most profoundly within. I pray you know what a precious creation you truly are.

I praise you, for I am fearfully
and wonderfully made.
Wonderful are your works;
my soul knows it very well.

PSALM 139:14 ESV

God loves us so much that He rescued us from the grip of anything else that promises to satisfy but won't.

RUTH CHOU SIMONS

For more
inspiration,
scan here:

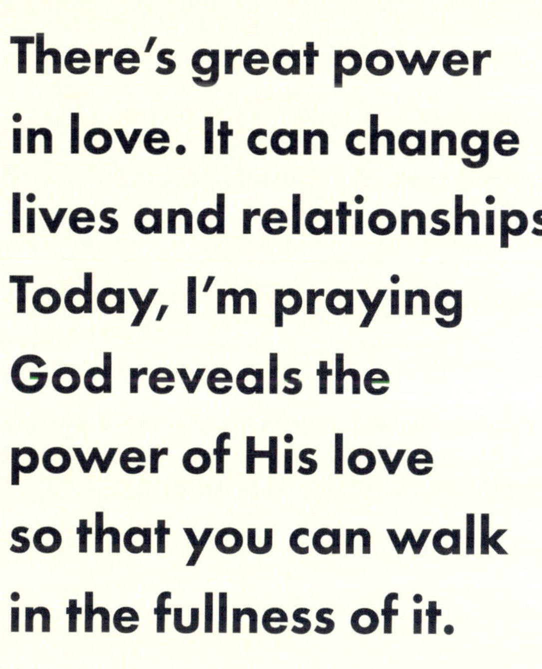

We have this treasure in jars of clay, to show that the surpassing power belongs to God and not to us.

II CORINTHIANS 4:7 ESV

God wants to win you not by exercising His power, but His love.

STEVEN CHOPADE

DaySpring

For more
inspiration,
scan here:

You are worthy. I asked God to let you know how much He loves and delights in you today.

Long before He laid down
earth's foundations, He had us in mind,
had settled on us as the focus of His love,
to be made whole and holy by His love.

EPHESIANS 1:4–6 THE MESSAGE

The peace of our souls does not have to
rise and fall with unpredictable people or situations.
Our feelings will shift, of course.
People do affect us. But the peace of our souls
can be tethered to all that God is.

LYSA TERKEURST

DaySpring

For more
inspiration,
scan here:

I am praying for you to sense God's love every minute of every day, knowing that you are cherished and valued by the One Most High.

"My love won't walk away from you,
My covenant commitment of peace
won't fall apart." The GOD who
has compassion on you says so.
ISAIAH 54:10 THE MESSAGE

Remember who you are. Don't compromise for anyone, for any reason. You are a child of the Almighty God. Live that truth.
LYSA TERKEURST

For more
inspiration,
scan here:

Today, I prayed that you would be reminded of God's miracle-working power.

You are the God
who works wonders;
you have made known
your might among the peoples.
PSALM 77:14 ESV

Where there is great love
there are always miracles.
WILLA CATHER

For more
inspiration,
scan here:

Love is like a ribbon, weaving in and out, bringing color to all it touches. Today, I prayed that God would show you what a colorful contribution you're making to all you come in contact with.

Beloved, if God so loved us,
we also ought to love one another.
I JOHN 4:11 ESV

When we show love to others God's presence is with us.
LINDA EVANS SHEPHERD

DaySpring

For more
inspiration,
scan here:

Look at you,
making the most
of every opportunity!
You're a real go-getter
who gets things done.
I pray that God's love
strengthens and encourages
you as you keep up
the good work!

Watch your step. Use your head.
Make the most of every chance you get.

EPHESIANS 5:16 THE MESSAGE

This is our time on the history line of God. This is it.
What will we do with the one deep exhale of God on this earth?
For we are but a vapor and we have to make it count.
We're on. Direct us, Lord, and get us on our feet.

BETH MOORE

DaySpring

For more
inspiration,
scan here:

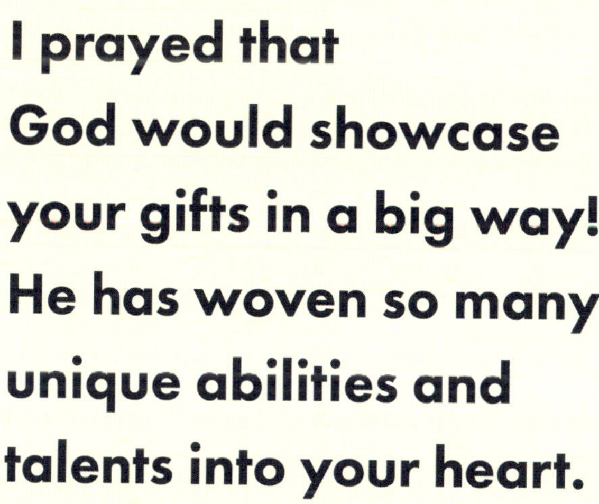

We have different gifts,
according to the grace
given to each of us.

ROMANS 12:6 NIV

God calls you to use all your gifts, talents and influence to serve others. Fight the lie that her talents are better than yours. Fight the lie that God can't use you for His Kingdom. Take inventory of your life, and prayerfully consider all the things God has given you to steward: your gifts, talents, influence, power and resources.

JAMIE IVEY

For more
inspiration,
scan here:

I prayed that God would remind you that He's singing and dancing over you. You make His heart very, very happy.

The LORD your God is with you,
the Mighty Warrior who saves.
He will take great delight in you;
in His love He will no longer rebuke you,
but will rejoice over you with singing.

ZEPHANIAH 3:17 NIV

Think of the purest, most all-consuming love you can imagine.
Now multiply that love by an infinite amount—
that is the measure of God's love for you.

DIETER F. UCHTDORF

For more
inspiration,
scan here:

I'm praying God will fill you with love and peace as you explore new avenues. You have incredible gifts to share with the world!

"See, I am doing a new thing!
Now it springs up; do you not perceive it?
I am making a way in the wilderness
and streams in the wasteland."

ISAIAH 43:19 NIV

Only you and the Lord know the dry and empty places in your soul. Are you ready to believe He is doing something new for you this year?

LIZ CURTIS HIGGS

DaySpring

For more
inspiration,
scan here:

God created you with purpose. I pray you'll experience His love by tapping into all the amazing characteristics, gifts, and passions that He has placed in your heart.

Every good and perfect gift
is from above, coming down from
the Father of the heavenly lights,
who does not change like shifting shadows.

JAMES 1:17 NIV

Whatever your unique gift, embrace it. Receive it. Rip off the paper and use it for His glory!

DORINA LAZO GILMORE-YOUNG

DaySpring

For more inspiration, scan here:

My prayer is that you rest in the assurance of His vast love for you.

Remind me each morning
of Your constant love,
for I put my trust in You.
My prayers go up to You;
show me the way I should go.

PSALM 143:8 GNT

Nothing binds me to my Lord like
a strong belief in His changeless love.

CHARLES H. SPURGEON

DaySpring

For more
inspiration,
scan here:

I'm praising God for you today! He truly did something amazing when He created you—just the way you are.

Then God said, "Let us make human beings in our image, to be like us."

GENESIS 1:26 NLT

God's asking me to be the thing He's already created me to be. And He's asking you to be the thing He's already created you to be. He doesn't tell the snow to thaw and become rain, or the rain to freeze itself into snow. He says, essentially: Do your thing. Do the thing you love to do, what you've been created to do.

SHAUNA NIEQUIST

DaySpring

For more inspiration, scan here:

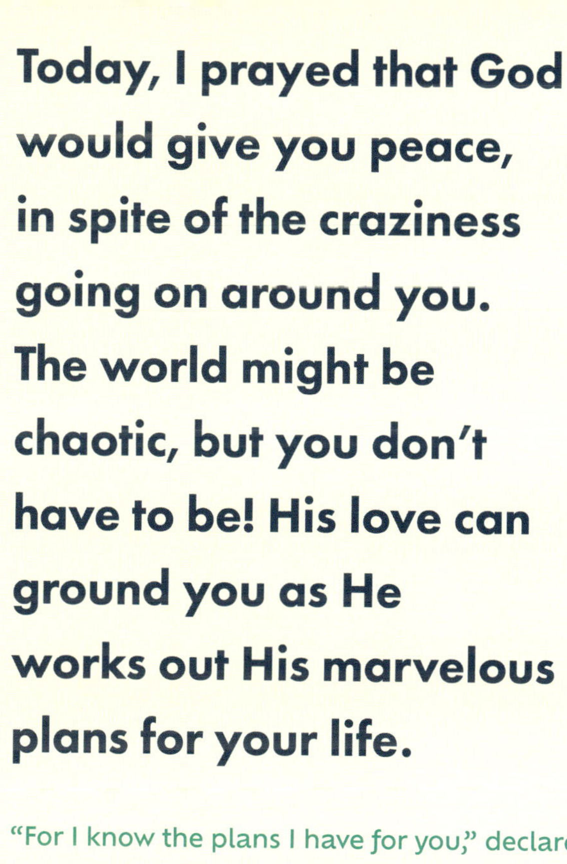

Today, I prayed that God would give you peace, in spite of the craziness going on around you. The world might be chaotic, but you don't have to be! His love can ground you as He works out His marvelous plans for your life.

"For I know the plans I have for you," declares the LORD, "plans for welfare and not for evil, to give you a future and a hope."
JEREMIAH 29:11 ESV

God is unchanging in His love. He loves you. He has a plan for your life. Don't let the newspaper headlines frighten you. God is still sovereign; He's still on the throne.
BILLY GRAHAM

For more
inspiration,
scan here:

As I prayed today,
I asked God to remind
you of His faithfulness.
He won't let you down.
His love for you
is unfailing.

Know therefore that the LORD your God is God,
the faithful God who keeps covenant
and steadfast love with those who love him
and keep his commandments,
to a thousand generations.
DEUTERONOMY 7:9 ESV

Throw yourself upon God's faithfulness
as you do upon your bed,
bringing all your weariness to His dear rest.
CHARLES SPURGEON

DaySpring

For more inspiration, scan here:

God's love knows no boundaries. It fills every corner of your heart. It guides every step of your journey. Today, I prayed you would experience this amazing love like never before.

"I have loved you, My people,
with an everlasting love.
With unfailing love
I have drawn you to Myself."

JEREMIAH 31:3 NLT

There is no pit so deep that
God's love is not deeper still.

CORRIE TEN BOOM

I'm praying you'll be strengthened by God's unshakable love as you face the battles ahead.

We are more than conquerors
through him who loved us.

ROMANS 8:37 ESV

God wants to give us roots and wings—
so we can grow deep into His love
and soar high into His call.

JENNIFER DUKES LEE

DaySpring

For more inspiration, scan here:

I'm praying you'll experience God's love in the beauty of creation today.

Let the heavens be glad, and the earth rejoice!
Let the sea and everything in it shout His praise!
Let the fields and their crops burst out with joy!
Let the trees of the forest sing for joy.

PSALM 96:11–12 NLT

We need to find God, and He cannot be found in noise and restlessness. God is the friend of silence. See how nature—trees, flowers, grass—grows in silence; see the stars, the moon and the sun, how they move in silence. . . . We need silence to be able to touch souls.

MOTHER TERESA

DaySpring

For more inspiration, scan here:

When I prayed for you, I asked God to remind you that His plans—born out of love for you—are perfect. He's got great things ahead for you.

I am sure of this, that he who began a good work in you will bring it to completion at the day of Jesus Christ.

PHILIPPIANS 1:6 ESV

God's plans for you are better than any plans you have for yourself. So don't be afraid of God's will, even if it's different from yours.

GREG LAURIE

DaySpring

For more inspiration, scan here:

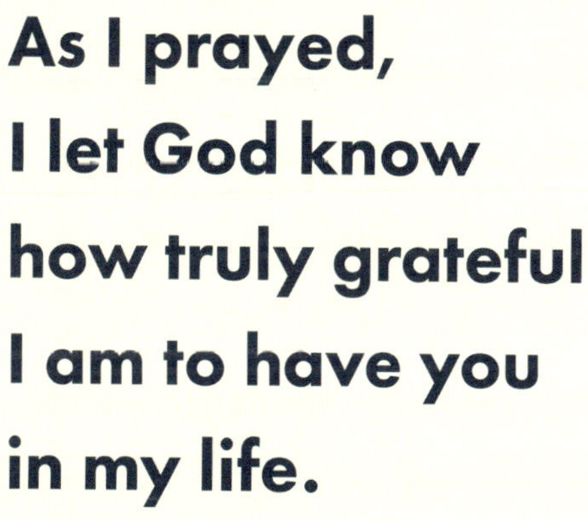

A man of many companions
may come to ruin,
but there is a friend
who sticks closer than a brother.
PROVERBS 18:24 ESV

Love is but the discovery of ourselves in others,
and the delight in the recognition.
ALEXANDER SMITH

For more
inspiration,
scan here:

God sees your efforts, friend. Today, I prayed that you would feel His love surrounding you, strengthening you, and reminding you that every step is valued by Him.

Let's not get tired of doing what is good.
At just the right time we will reap a harvest
of blessing if we don't give up.

GALATIANS 6:9 NLT

May God remind us daily—no matter what kind of obstacles
we face—that we are loved and empowered
by the One who brought the universe into existence
with the mere sound of His voice.
Nothing is impossible for Him.

BETH MOORE

DaySpring

For more
inspiration,
scan here:

Today I prayed that God would infuse you with His love, His strength, His joy, and His courage to continue down the road you're walking. He's bigger than any mountains you're facing, I promise.

Love suffers long and is kind;
love does not envy; love does not parade itself, is not puffed up; does not behave rudely, does not seek its own, is not provoked, thinks no evil.

I CORINTHIANS 13:4–5 NKJV

Your mess is not too big for God.

SHEILA WALSH

DaySpring

For more
inspiration,
scan here:

I prayed for you today and asked God to place the perfect people in your life, ones who will bring a smile to your face.

No one has ever seen God,
but if we love one another,
God lives in union with us, and
His love is made perfect in us.
I JOHN 4:12 GNT

We heal up through being loved,
and through loving others.
JEANETTE WINTERSON

DaySpring

For more inspiration, scan here:

Before you were ever born, God knew you and loved you. I asked Him to remind you of that today. You've always been valuable to Him!

You created every part of me;
You put me together in my mother's womb.
I praise You because You are to be feared;
all You do is strange and wonderful.
I know it with all my heart.

PSALM 139:13–14 GNT

You are the object of God's affection.
He has relentlessly pursued and will continue to pursue you.

KIA STEPHENS

For more
inspiration,
scan here:

Today, I asked God to provide time in your day for stillness and rest. My prayer is that you will feel His love surround you, refresh your spirit, and renew your strength.

"Abide in me, and I in you.
As the branch cannot bear fruit by itself,
unless it abides in the vine,
neither can you, unless you abide in me."

JOHN 15:4 ESV

The first secret to loving others is to immerse yourself in a love relationship with God the Father, God the Son, and God the Holy Spirit—and abide there.

ANNE GRAHAM LOTZ

For more
inspiration,
scan here:

I pray you'll experience God's love in unexpected places and in the simple things today.

This is the day the LORD has made.
We will rejoice and be glad in it.
PSALM 118:24 NLT

Wherever you are in life, know that
God pursued us first because
we are important to Him.
He made us in His image.
Read what He has to say.
You will find the best Dad
on a mission to rescue His children.
LINDSAY VOSSMAN BRASHEAR

DaySpring

For more inspiration, scan here:

I asked God to fill you with joy as you encounter His love in countless ways today.

I pray that God, the source of hope,
will fill you completely with joy and peace
because you trust in Him.

ROMANS 15:13 NLT

Joy is the infallible proof
of the presence of God.

MADELEINE L'ENGLE

For more
inspiration,
scan here:

How you view yourself is so important! Today, I asked God to remind you that He views you as beautiful in His sight!

You are altogether beautiful,
my darling; there is no flaw in you.
SONG OF SOLOMON 4:7 NIV

People often say that "beauty is in the eye of the beholder," and I say that the most liberating thing about beauty is realizing that you are the beholder. This empowers us to find beauty in places where others have not dared to look, including inside ourselves.
SALMA HAYEK

DaySpring

For more inspiration, scan here:

I asked God to remind you how happy you make Him!

A glad heart
makes a cheerful face,
but by sorrow of heart
the spirit is crushed.
PROVERBS 15:13 ESV

When you enjoy your life,
you bring JOY to the One
who gave it to you.
HOLLEY GERTH

DaySpring

For more inspiration, scan here:

I prayed that you would experience God's love in a variety of ways today—maybe through the kindness of others, the joy of serving, or the peace that comes with resting in His embrace.

You, Lord, are a compassionate and gracious God, slow to anger, abounding in love and faithfulness.

PSALM 86:15 NIV

God's love never ceases. Never . . . God doesn't love us less if we fail or more if we succeed. God's love never ceases.

MAX LUCADO

DaySpring

For more inspiration, scan here:

Today, God wants to remind you that He delights in you! He plans to pour out blessings on you that you can't even imagine!

Delight yourself in the LORD,
and he will give you
the desires of your heart.

PSALM 37:4 ESV

However many blessings we expect from God,
His infinite liberality will always exceed
all our wishes and our thoughts.

JOHN CALVIN

DaySpring

For more inspiration, scan here:

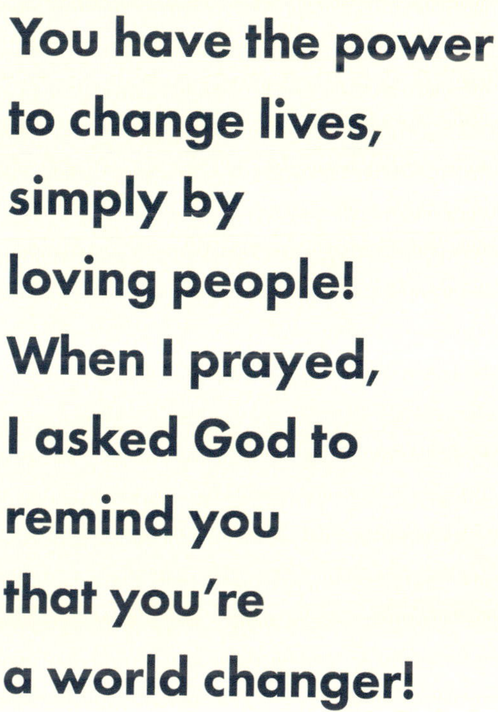

You have the power to change lives, simply by loving people! When I prayed, I asked God to remind you that you're a world changer!

Let brotherly love continue.

HEBREWS 13:1 ESV

Love me when I least deserve it,
because that's when I really need it.

SWEDISH PROVERB

For more
inspiration,
scan here:

Today, I prayed for you to encounter God's love, not just in the big moments, but also in the small, everyday acts.

God is love.

I JOHN 4:16 NIV

You may not be able to measure God's love, but you can certainly experience it.

DILLON BURROUGHS

DaySpring

For more inspiration, scan here:

As I prayed for you, God nudged me to remind you that He loves every part of you—flawed and unflawed.

God shows his love for us
in that while we were still sinners,
Christ died for us.
ROMANS 5:8 ESV

God's love is bigger than our failures and stronger than any chains that bind us.
JENNIFER ROTHSCHILD

DaySpring

For more
inspiration,
scan here:

I prayed that you would find rest in the truth that you are deeply loved by God—unconditionally and forever.

Truly my soul finds rest in God.

PSALM 62:1 NIV

If you look at the world, you'll be distressed.
If you look within, you'll be depressed.
If you look at God, you'll be at rest.

CORRIE TEN BOOM

DaySpring

For more
inspiration,
scan here:

I prayed that God would remind you how much He loves having you in His big beautiful family!

See how much the Father has loved us! His love is so great that we are called God's children—and so, in fact, we are.

I JOHN 3:1 GNT

Though we are imperfect, He loves us perfectly. Though we may feel lost and without compass, God's love encompasses us completely. . . . He loves every one of us, even those who are flawed, rejected, awkward, sorrowful, or broken.

DIETER F. UCHTDORF

DaySpring

For more inspiration, scan here:

Today, I prayed that you would sense God's love carrying you through life's ups and downs.

Every detail in our lives of love
for God is worked into something good.

ROMANS 8:28 THE MESSAGE

The only love that won't disappoint you
is one that can't change, that can't be lost,
that is not based on the ups and downs of life
or of how well you live. It is something that not even death
can take away from you. God's love is the only thing like that.

TIMOTHY KELLER

DaySpring

For more
inspiration,
scan here:

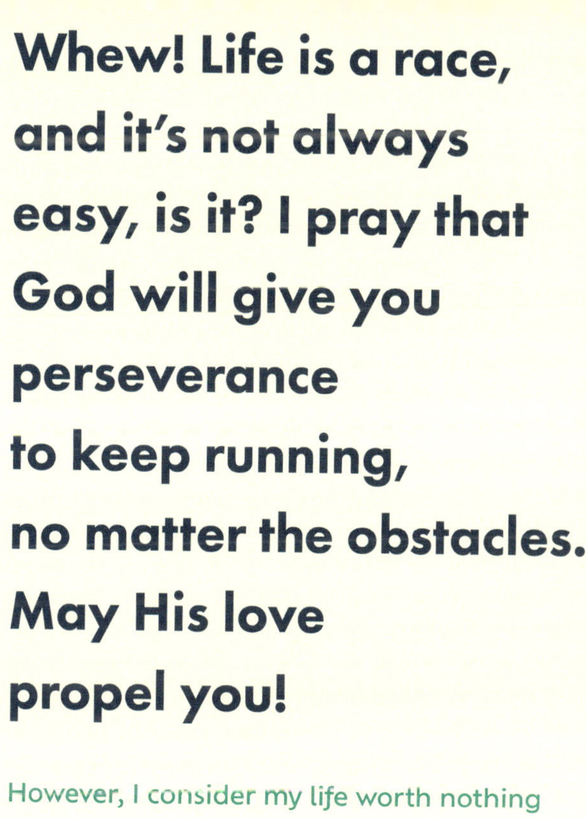

Whew! Life is a race, and it's not always easy, is it? I pray that God will give you perseverance to keep running, no matter the obstacles. May His love propel you!

However, I consider my life worth nothing to me; my only aim is to finish the race and complete the task the Lord Jesus has given me—the task of testifying to the good news of God's grace.

ACTS 20:24 NIV

Obstacles are those frightful things you see when you take your eyes off the goal.

HANNAH MORE

DaySpring

For more
inspiration,
scan here:

I pray that God's love provides a strong foundation for you to stand on during this bumpy road. His love is strong, powerful, and never-failing.

The Lord is my strength and shield.
I trust Him, and He helps me.
I am very happy.
And I praise Him with my song.

PSALM 28:7 ICB

No matter what storms are raging all around,
you'll stand firm if you stand on His love.

CHARLES STANLEY

DaySpring

For more
inspiration,
scan here:

Today, I prayed for you to experience God's love— a love that heals, transforms, and empowers.

He heals the brokenhearted
and binds up their wounds.
PSALM 147:3 NIV

God loves to take people from broken backgrounds
and surprise them with possibilities.
LYSA TERKEURST

DaySpring

For more
inspiration,
scan here:

God knows you and loves you . . . and He doesn't expect perfection. I prayed that God would free you from any pressure to do anything in order to earn His love—because His love is already yours.

For by grace you have been saved
through faith. And this is not your
own doing; it is the gift of God,
not a result of works,
so that no one may boast.

EPHESIANS 2:8–9 ESV

The only way to break the chains of fear and doubt is to know in your heart that God loves you—no matter what.

JOYCE MEYER

DaySpring

For more inspiration, scan here:

I asked God to remind you that He's a good, good Father. His love can be trusted.

I remain confident of this:
I will see the goodness of the LORD
in the land of the living.
PSALM 27:13 NIV

We should be astonished at the goodness of God, stunned that He should bother to call us by name, our mouths wide open at His love, bewildered that at this very moment we are standing on holy ground.
BRENNAN MANNING

DaySpring

For more inspiration, scan here:

I prayed for God's love to fully mend your whole heart today. He understands the pain that still lingers. May you find true rest in His arms.

Praise be to the God and Father of our Lord Jesus Christ, the Father of compassion and the God of all comfort, who comforts us in all our troubles, so that we can comfort those in any trouble with the comfort we ourselves receive from God.

II CORINTHIANS 1:3–4 NIV

For God to mend your broken heart you must give Him ALL the pieces. You can't hold any back.

RICK WARREN

I pray that God's love will overcome all your fears and concerns today, drawing you into His peace and rest.

There is no fear in love.
But perfect love drives out fear.
1 JOHN 4:18 NIV

Jesus invites us to abide in His love.
That means to dwell with all that I am in Him.
It is an invitation to a total belonging, to full intimacy,
to an unlimited being-with. The light of the Spirit
reveals to us that love conquers all fear.
HENRI NOUWEN

For more
inspiration,
scan here:

Today, I pray that you will sense God's loving presence. He's right there with you, in the midst of the trials you're going through.

I will take refuge
in the shadow of Your wings
until the disaster has passed.

PSALM 57:1 NIV

God is mighty. God is caring. God is worthy of praise. God is loving. God is able. God is in control. Nothing takes God by surprise. Some sweet reminders to soak in before falling asleep tonight.

LYSA TERKEURST

DaySpring

For more
inspiration,
scan here:

I pray that you will rest easy in God's immeasurable love today.

I pray that you, being rooted and
established in love, may have power,
together with all the Lord's holy people,
to grasp how wide and long and high and
deep is the love of Christ, and to know
this love that surpasses knowledge—
that you may be filled to the measure
of all the fullness of God.

EPHESIANS 3:17–19 NIV

You may not be able to measure God's love, but you can certainly experience it.

DILLON BURROUGHS

DaySpring

For more inspiration, scan here:

I prayed and asked God to lavish you with good gifts! His love for you is boundless, and He loves to pour out blessings.

Every good and perfect gift
is from above, coming down from
the Father of the heavenly lights,
who does not change
like shifting shadows.

JAMES 1:17 NIV

The love of God is not created—it is His nature.

OSWALD CHAMBERS

DaySpring

For more
inspiration,
scan here:

I prayed that God's love would propel you forward, giving you the courage needed to take steps of faith even when the path feels uncertain.

If God is for us, who can be against us?
ROMANS 8:31 NIV

Don't let not knowing how it'll end keep you from beginning. Uncertainty chases us out into the open where God is waiting.
BOB GOFF

DaySpring

For more
inspiration,
scan here:

It was never up to you, sweet friend. Today I'm praying that you lean on the One who knows you best and loves you most.

Trust in the LORD
with all your heart and
lean not on your own understanding.
PROVERBS 3:5 NIV

The next time you find yourself alone in a dark alley facing the undeniables of life, don't cover them with a blanket, or ignore them with a nervous grin. Don't turn up the TV and pretend they aren't there. Instead, stand still, whisper His name, and listen. He is nearer than you think.

MAX LUCADO

DaySpring

For more
inspiration,
scan here:

How long will God go on loving you? Forever, my friend. Nothing you do can separate you from Him. Today, I pray you will enjoy the reassurance this truth brings.

Give thanks to the God of heaven,
for his steadfast love endures forever.
PSALM 136:26 ESV

God's love looks for those who feel unlovely,
desiring to make them beautiful again.
NATALIE GRANT

I prayed that you would find comfort in knowing you will always be loved with the purest, most unconditional love possible—a love that will never fail or fade.

Do you think anyone
is going to be able to
drive a wedge between us
and Christ's love for us? There is no way!

ROMANS 8:38–39 THE MESSAGE

To know God's love is indeed heaven on earth.

J. I. PACKER

DaySpring

For more inspiration, scan here:

My prayer for you, as you face this day, is that you will see that God is working all things together for your good. That's how much He loves you!

[Love] does not rejoice in iniquity,
but rejoices in the truth; bears all things,
believes all things, hopes all things,
endures all things.

I CORINTHIANS 13:6–7 NKJV

Because God loves us, He gives us lyrics to sing when our hearts can't form words.

JENNIFER ROTHSCHILD

DaySpring

For more
inspiration,
scan here: